# Have You Heard?

Lesley Jane

Illustrated by Mitch Vane

CLEEVE PRIMARY

GW01463857

**Momentum**
Have You Heard?

First published in Great Britain in 1998 by

Folens Publishers
Albert House
Apex Business Centre
Boscombe Road
Dunstable
Beds LU5 4RL

© 1998 Momentum developed by Barrie Publishing Pty Limited
Suite 513, 89 High St, Kew, Vic 3101, Australia

Lesley Jane hereby asserts her moral right to be identified as the
author of this work in accordance with the Copyright, Designs and
Patents Act 1988.
© 1998 Folens Ltd. on behalf of the author.
Illustrations copyright Mitch Vane

All rights reserved. No part of this publication may be reproduced
or transmitted in any form or by any means, electronic or
mechanical, including photocopying, recording or any information
storage and retrieval system, without written permission from the
publisher.

British Library Cataloguing in Publication Data.
A Catalogue record for this book is available from the British
Library

ISBN 1 86202 405 7

Designed by Tom Kurema
Printed in Singapore by PH Productions Pte Ltd

It was a lazy, hazy day. Unseen insects hummed in the bushes. Still, warm air lay over Siesta Avenue. Norma Fisher was in her garden with her black cat, Buzz, who had spent the morning hunting. His thick fur was tangled, and Norma needed to hold Buzz quite firmly to groom him.

In the distance a door slammed. There was the sound of an excited dog, and a boy on a bike skidded past Norma's house. He rang his bicycle bell loudly and disappeared across Siesta Avenue, then down Paperbark Place.

The blast of the bell was too much for Buzz. He made a wild leap to escape Norma's grip. He didn't stop moving until he was high in the apple tree with every one of his hairs standing on end. Norma tried to coax him down.

"Here, Buzzy, Buzzy," she called, but the cat didn't budge. He hung on tightly, yowling low in his throat. His ears were laid flat and he glared at Norma with wide, wild eyes.

"I'll have to get the ladder," sighed Norma.

Mavis Brown, Norma's friend,
was at the clothesline. She saw
Norma carrying the ladder
and was curious. She called
over the fence to her
friend, "Is anything
wrong?"

"Buzz is stuck in the
apple tree," said
Norma. "That bicycle
bell gave him a fright,
and now I need to
climb up to rescue
him."

"Take care," said
Mavis. She watched
nervously as Norma
tried to reach Buzz.

"It's no good. He's too
high," said Norma. "I'll have
to think of something else."
Mavis watched until Norma
reached the ground safely. She knew
her friend was upset so she decided to prepare
a treat to cheer her up. But first she had to
finish hanging out the clothes.

Old Ted Potts was working in his garden. When he finished planting the seedlings, he stood up and stretched. He saw Mavis Brown at her clothesline and raised his old gardening hat.

"How are you today, Mavis?" he asked.

"I've just had a fright," shouted Mavis. Ted Potts was a little hard of hearing.

"A fight!" gasped Ted.

"No, a fright," yelled Mavis. "Norma climbed a ladder to get her cat. He was in the tree."

"Who was that? Norma in a tree, you say?" Ted Potts put a hand to his good ear.

"I was sure she would fall," roared Mavis. She was wishing she hadn't stopped to talk.

"Fall, you say." Ted Potts could not believe his ears.

Mavis nodded at Ted and made a quick getaway. She saw how worried he looked, so as she left she bellowed, "There is no need for alarm."

"Her arm!" said Ted Potts. "Poor Norma. Broken her arm. She's probably gone to the hospital!"

Ted was very upset. He was trying to think of a way to cheer up Norma when he saw Angie Lo arrive home. She lived next door.

"We won!" she called across the fence. She had been playing in the basketball finals. She waved her medallion.

Ted said, "Congratulations," but he looked worried. So Angie asked him what was wrong.

"Sad news," he said. "Poor Norma Fisher fell out of a tree. She broke her arm and was taken to the hospital."

"Oh, dear," said Angie. "I had better tell my mother."

"I wonder who's looking after Norma's cat," said Angie's mother when she heard the news. "Go to the supermarket and get some cat food, Angie. We'll take care of Buzz."

She gave Angie enough money for the very best cat food. Then she phoned her friend, Sylvia Gonzales.

Sylvia was watching an old movie on television. She was only half listening to what Angie's mother was saying.

"Oh, that's terrible," said Sylvia. "No . . . That's so sad . . . I didn't even hear the ambulance siren."

"What siren?" called Harry Gonzales from the kitchen. He was making a batch of his special tomato chutney. The hot vinegar fumes made him very light-headed.

Sylvia put her hand over the mouthpiece and yelled, "That nice Miss Fisher has been rushed to the hospital, Harry."

"Was she hurt at home?" asked Harry.

"I think so," said his wife.

Harry Gonzales was wrapped in clouds of spicy steam. He thought about what a dangerous place the home could be. Every year careless people injured themselves in their kitchens. Kitchens are full of sharp things that cut and things that burn if you don't take care. He shuddered as he remembered his own close call. Last winter he had lost his eyebrows when the fat in a frying pan exploded into flames.

"Was she hurt in the kitchen?" he called to his wife.

But Sylvia was not listening. She was watching her movie. Harry repeated his question.

"Yes, yes," said Sylvia, hoping he would stop interrupting.

"Don't tell me it was a fat fire!" called Harry. Sylvia gave a grunt. Harry took that to mean yes.

"Dear, oh dear," said Harry Gonzales. "Fat fires make a terrible mess. Poor Miss Fisher. I'll go and help with the clean-up."

He stirred the chutney one more time, turned off the gas, and went to get some heavy-duty cleaner from the garden shed.

Sam Watson from the house next door heard Harry banging around in his shed. He was curious to know what was going on.

"Hello, Sam," said Harry. "There has been a fire at Miss Fisher's . . . "

But Sam was already moving. He had heard just one word – FIRE! – and that was enough. Here he was, with only one week as a member of the Volunteer Fire Brigade, and there was an emergency already!

He imagined the worst – towering flames, heat and noise. He raced across the road to the Petersons' house. They were all fellow Fire Brigade members.

The Petersons were quick to respond to the emergency. They began filling buckets with water while Sam wrapped wet towels around their heads.

Everyone arrived at Norma's house at the same time. Mavis Brown had a plate of fresh muffins to cheer up her friend. Ted Potts had picked a huge bunch of his best flowers. He was going to catch the bus to the hospital, but when he saw Mavis Brown opening Norma's gate, he guessed that the patient must be at home.

Angie Lo and her mother had cat food for Buzz. Harry Gonzales had some heavy-duty cleaner, and his wife was carrying some rubber gloves.

Sam Watson and the Petersons moved quickly up the rear with their buckets of water. Joe Peterson was wearing diving gear in case he needed to rescue Norma from her smoke-filled house. It was hard for him to see where he was going through the mask.

When Sam saw the crowd of people near Norma's gate, he yelled, "Stand back! Let me through!"

Everyone became alarmed and began running into Norma's backyard. There they found Norma reading and enjoying the warm, lazy, hazy day. Buzz was sleeping in her lap. She had coaxed him out of the tree with a bowl of milk. Buzz jumped in fright when everyone came crashing through the gate. The moment they saw Norma they knew she was not hurt or in danger. Their concern turned to anger. They looked at one another to find who had been telling stories. Only Joe Peterson was safe from the suspicious glares. His mask had fogged up.

Norma took command of the situation. She brought out more chairs and a jug of homemade lemonade.

Before long, everyone was enjoying the delicious muffins and icy-cold lemonade and laughing about what had happened.